CONFIDENT CONFIDENCE

From Self-Doubt to Unshakable: The Proven Path to Building Confidence That Doesn't Break Under Pressure

TYRUS J. HINTON

Copyright © 2025 by Tyrus J. Hinton
www.tyrusjhinton.com

All rights reserved.
No part of this book may be reproduced or used in any manner without the written permission of the copyright owner, except for the use of quotations in a book review.

Book Project Management:
Start Write | Raindrop Creative, INC.

Editor:
Tiara Brown

Book Cover Creative Direction:
Tyrus J. Hinton

Book Cover Creative Design:
Donovan Purvey

FIRST EDITION | RALEIGH, NC

ISBN: 978-0-9987700-7-9

Dedication

To my children, grandchildren, great-grandchildren, and the generations to follow:

*May you all be filled with **Confident Confidence;***

May you never lack the ability to confidently accomplish anything you put your hands to;

May you always know that you are enough, and that you have precisely what it takes to be the best;

May your presence light up and command every room – from the classroom to the boardroom;

This book is my gift to you, a reminder that the confidence you carry will always be your greatest inheritance.

Table of Contents

Dedication		3
Introduction		7
Chapter One:	Confidence Under Attack	11
Chapter Two:	Breaking Free from Other People's Approval	21
Chapter Three:	Dream the Impossible Dream	29
Chapter Four:	The Confidence Contract–Do the Work	37
Chapter Five:	Fear, Failure, and the Courage to Try Again	43
Chapter Six:	The Confidence Cost	51
Chapter Seven:	Rejection is Direction	57
Chapter Eight:	The Confidence Economy	65
Chapter Nine:	The Comparison Trap	71
Chapter Ten:	The Confidence Blueprint	77
Chapter Eleven:	The Weight of Confidence	85
Chapter Twelve:	Confident Confidence in High-Pressure Environments	95
Conclusion:	Living with Confident Confidence	105

Introduction

What if confidence wasn't just a feeling—but a skill you could master? In a world full of pressure, comparison, and constant change, confidence has become one of the most valuable assets a person can have. But not all confidence is created equal. Some people have confidence only when things are going well. Others cling to it until the first sign of rejection or failure sends them crumbling to pieces.

This book introduces you to something substantial—**Confident Confidence**—the kind that doesn't crack under criticism, wilt under pressure, or disappear when the odds are against you. Inside these pages, you'll discover:

- **The Mindset Shift**: How to move from hoping things will work out to knowing you can make them work.
- **The Power of Resilience**: Why failure, rejection, and risk are not threats to confidence but building blocks for it.
- **The Truth About Validation**: How to silence the critics, quiet the noise of comparison, and stop living for other people's approval.
- **Confidence in Health**: Why weight loss, energy, and appearance can unlock new levels of confidence–and how your physical health impacts your ability to show up fully at work, at home, and in relationships.
- **Thriving Under Pressure**: How to build and maintain confidence in cutthroat, competitive environments–corporate, nonprofit, or entrepreneurial–where calm and clarity can set you apart and elevate you above the noise.
- **Strategies for Business and Life**: Practical tools to help you lead confidently, build

stronger relationships, and seize opportunities with clarity and courage.

Whether you are an entrepreneur shaping your brand, a professional climbing the corporate ladder, or someone ready to break free from self-doubt, this book will provide you with the mental framework and real-world examples to build lasting confidence. When you finish reading, you won't just feel inspired for the moment—you will walk away with the mindset, strategies, and confidence to create lasting success in every area of your life.

Welcome to **Confident Confidence.**

Your future self will thank you.

CHAPTER ONE:
Confidence Under Attack

Why Your Belief in Yourself is the First Thing the World Will Try to Destroy

If you're aiming to build something significant—whether it's a business, a brand, a career, or a movement—prepare yourself: your confidence will come under attack. It happens to every visionary, every innovator, every ambitious leader who dares to push beyond the familiar. The attack might come from critics, from the marketplace, from loved ones who "mean well," or even from your own self-doubt whispering in the quiet hours of the night. But make no mistake—if you're aiming to do anything remarkable, your confidence will be tested.

Theodore Roosevelt captured this perfectly when he said: *"It is not the critic who counts; not the man who points out how the strong man stumbles, or where the doer of deeds could have done them better. The credit belongs to the man who is actually in the arena...who strives valiantly, who errs, who comes short again and again...but who does so daring greatly, so that his place shall never be with those cold and timid souls who neither know victory nor defeat."* The people who never risk anything will always have the loudest opinions.

Visionaries Attract Attacks

History is filled with stories of innovators who were told they were crazy before the world called them geniuses.

- **Dr. Seuss** was rejected by over 20 publishers before his first book was published. Today, his works have sold hundreds of millions of copies worldwide.

- **Walt Disney** was turned down by more than 300 bankers who thought Mickey Mouse was absurd and Disneyland was impossible. Today, Disney is one of the most powerful entertainment empires in the world.
- **Oprah Winfrey** was fired from her first job as a TV anchor because she "wasn't fit for television."
- **Michael Jordan** was cut from his high school basketball team before becoming one of the most iconic athletes of all time.

Every one of them had something bigger than ordinary confidence. Ordinary confidence hopes things will work out. **Confident Confidence** says: *This will work because I will make it work.* That's the difference. Ordinary confidence crumbles after rejection. Confident Confidence gets stronger.

Early Attacks Hit the Hardest

For many of us, the first attacks on our confidence came long before adulthood—often in childhood, when we were too young to separate someone else's pain from our own potential. Sometimes it was a teacher who doubted us. Sometimes, a parent whose own wounds leaked into their words. Sometimes, peers mocked dreams they couldn't understand. And those early words leave marks. They form the soundtrack of self-doubt that plays on repeat later in life.

I know this personally. My earliest memories include hearing phrases like *"You'll never be anything,"* and *"You're just not smart enough."* When you hear that young enough, and often enough, it begins to feel like the truth, but here's what life eventually taught me: **Criticism reveals more about the critic than it does about you.** People speak from their own ceilings. They hand you the limits they've accepted for themselves.

Once I realized that, everything changed. Their words no longer defined me.

The Trap of Playing Small

Not everyone responds to early attacks the same way. Some fight harder. Others shrink back, choosing safety over visibility. This mindset is what I call *playing small*—settling for less than your potential because risk feels terrifying. If you stay quiet, maybe you won't be criticized. If you never try, you'll never fail. If you hide, you can't get hurt.

But playing small comes with a cost:

- You trade ambition for comfort.
- You avoid judgment but also forfeit growth.
- You protect your ego but sacrifice your future.

And worst of all, you risk building a life so "safe" that it never really feels like living.

Fear of failure often disguises itself as wisdom. It whispers questions like:

- *What will people say about me if I fail?*
- *What if I'm not as talented as I think?*
- *What if I try, but embarrass myself?*

Here's the truth: those questions never go away. The confident learn to act *while afraid*.

Marketing, Media, and Manufactured Insecurity

There's another reason confidence is so fragile today: we are bombarded with messages designed to make us feel inadequate. The entire advertising industry runs on one formula:

1. To tell you something is missing in your life.
2. To agitate the pain of not having it.
3. To sell you a solution.

Every commercial, every luxury brand, every influencer post on social media pushes the same narrative: *You're not enough until you buy what we're selling.* And their marketing often works. People buy the car, the bag, the house—only to find that emptiness isn't solved with a purchase. Confidence rooted in possessions isn't confidence at all. **Confident Confidence** says: *I bring value into the room because of who I am, not what I own.*

The Social Media Illusion

Social media has amplified the attack on self-worth. We now compare our real lives to other people's curated highlight reels.

- We see the romantic vacation photos, not the arguments before the trip.
- We see the business wins, not the sleepless nights behind the scenes.
- We see the luxury lifestyle, not the debt hiding beneath it.

Comparison will convince you that you're failing when, in fact, you're making progress. That's why I have a personal rule: **burn the**

highlight reel. Don't compare your behind-the-scenes to someone else's red-carpet moments. Build a life you actually enjoy when no one's watching.

Why This Matters

If someone can attack your confidence early enough, they can control the rest of your life. The critic on the outside eventually becomes the voice within. And once you believe that voice, you stop trying. You stop risking. You stop dreaming. That's why this book exists—to help you silence that voice for good.

The world doesn't just need confident people. It needs people with **Confident Confidence**—people so grounded in who they are and what they can do that no amount of rejection, criticism, or comparison can shake them.

Key Takeaways from Chapter One

- Visionaries attract attacks—it's a sign you're aiming higher than most.
- Ordinary confidence hopes; Confident Confidence decides.
- Early criticism plants seeds of self-doubt. Uproot them by separating other people's pain from your potential.
- Playing small protects your ego but sabotages your future.
- Advertising and social media foster insecurity—guard your mind.
- Build a life you enjoy offline, not just one that looks good online.

CHAPTER TWO:
Breaking Free from Other People's Approval

How to Stop Chasing Applause and Start Defining Success on Your Own Terms

The fastest way to lose yourself is to live for the approval of others. The fastest way to find yourself is to stop caring who claps. Success looks different for everyone. But for too many people, it isn't defined by fulfillment or freedom or impact—it's defined by how loudly other people applaud when they see it.

Here's the problem: if you live for the applause, you will eventually die from the silence. Confident Confidence begins where the need for validation ends. It's the moment you decide that your worth isn't up for a vote.

The Weight of Their Opinions

Critics always seem to have perfect attendance. They don't miss a game, a speech, a launch, or a post. And they have opinions about everything. Some of them genuinely want to protect you from disappointment. Others feel threatened when you rise because it challenges the excuses they've built around staying the same.

Either way, if you try to please everyone, you will spend your life spinning in circles:

- **If you succeed too loudly**, they'll call you arrogant.
- **If you fail too publicly**, they'll say they saw it coming.
- **If you win quietly**, they'll say you're not ambitious enough.

See the trap? It's rigged. This is the reason why the most confident people don't crave public approval. They crave internal alignment.

Don't Be the Best. Be the Only.

We live in a culture obsessed with competition:

- Who's the best singer?
- Who's the greatest athlete?
- Who's the richest entrepreneur?

But here's the truth: *the most successful people in the world stopped trying to be the best a long time ago.* They decided to be the only.

Bob Marley was not the most technically gifted singer of his era. But when you want the sound of freedom, soul, and sun-soaked rebellion, there is no substitute for Bob Marley. Whitney Houston wasn't competing with Madonna. Michael Jordan wasn't competing with Tiger Woods. They weren't even in the same lane. When you lean into your uniqueness, there is no competition. No one can beat you at being you.

The Tyranny of Comparison

Social media has made comparison an extreme sport. Someone else's promotion will make you question your career. Someone else's vacation will make you question your lifestyle. Someone else's highlight reel will make you question your whole existence. But comparison doesn't just steal joy—it strangles confidence.

Here's why: when your worth depends on outperforming someone else, you will always feel behind. There will always be someone younger, richer, fitter, or more "liked." Confident Confidence refuses to play this game. It doesn't measure success by likes, followers, or net worth flexes. It measures success by *alignment*—living in a way that matches your purpose, values, and potential.

No Competition in Your Lane

When you understand your lane, you stop competing and start creating. Too many businesses collapse because they start chasing trends instead of building on their strengths. The burger shop sees fried chicken trending and suddenly abandons the menu that made them famous.

It's the same with careers. Someone may see an influencer making money online and abandon the career they were born to master. However, when you know your lane, you stop chasing trends and start setting them. Confident Confidence says: *I don't have to be louder than you. I just have to be clear about me.*

When Love Feels Like Limitation

Here's where it gets tricky: sometimes the people who love you most are the ones who unintentionally limit you.

- The parent who says, *"Don't take risks. Just get a safe job."*
- The spouse who says, *"Why can't you just be happy with what you have?"*
- The friend who says, *"Don't set yourself up for disappointment."*

They mean well. They want to protect you. But protection rooted in fear always sounds like limitation.

They aren't trying to crush your dream—they're just terrified of watching you get hurt chasing it. Confident Confidence learns to separate love from agreement. Someone can love you deeply and still not believe in your vision. You have to decide which voice gets the final say.

Why You Must Stop Asking for Permission

Here's the secret nobody tells you: Every breakthrough looks reckless until it works. When Jeff Bezos started selling books online, traditional retailers thought he was ridiculous. When Elon Musk poured his money into electric cars, legacy automakers thought it was a hobby. When Netflix started mailing DVDs, Blockbuster laughed them out of the room. Nobody applauded them in the beginning. The approval came after the results. That's why waiting for permission is the slowest route to success.

Key Takeaways from Chapter Two

- Stop living for the applause, or you'll die from the silence.
- Competing for "best" is a trap. Own your lane— be the only.
- Comparison culture steals confidence. Alignment builds it.
- People who love you may project fear onto your dreams. Listen, but don't let it limit you.
- Stop asking for permission to be great. Results create the approval you're waiting for.

CHAPTER THREE:
Dream the Impossible Dream

Why Playing it Safe Costs More Than Dreaming Big

Somewhere between childhood and adulthood, most people stop dreaming. When we were kids, the world felt limitless. We believed we could become astronauts, athletes, artists, or entrepreneurs because nobody had told us it wasn't possible yet.

Then the voices came:

- *"Be realistic."*
- *"Get a safe job."*
- *"Don't set yourself up for disappointment."*

And little by little, the dream shrank. The tragedy? Most people don't even notice the moment they traded ambition for safety.

The Day Steve Harvey Was Told to Play Small

Steve Harvey tells the story of a sixth-grade teacher who asked the class to write down what they wanted to be when they grew up. Steve wrote: *"I want to be on TV."* When the teacher read his answer out loud, she didn't smile. She didn't encourage him. She called him to the front of the room and said, *"Steve, do you know anyone on TV? Has anyone in your family ever been on TV? No? Then be realistic. Write something believable."*

Steve Harvey was crushed. Today, Steve Harvey appears on TV seven days a week. And every Christmas, he sends that same teacher a flat-screen television so she can see exactly how wrong she was. The point of the matter is this:

The world will try to shrink your dreams to fit inside its comfort zone.

Why "Be Realistic" is Dream-Killing Advice

When someone says, *"Be realistic,"* what they often mean is:

- "Don't dream bigger than I can imagine."
- "Don't chase something I would be afraid to chase."
- "Don't make me uncomfortable by doing what I gave up on."

Most people aren't protecting you when they say this. They're protecting their own belief systems. Dreaming big threatens people who have made peace with living small.

The Internal Voice That Keeps You Safe… and Stuck

The problem is that over time, you don't need other people to discourage you anymore. Their voices become your voice.

- *"What if this doesn't work?"*
- *"What if I'm not good enough?"*
- *"What will people say if I fail?"*

That voice sounds rational. It calls itself wisdom. It disguises itself as responsibility. But most of the time, it's fear in a business suit. And if you listen to it long enough, you won't even try.

Dreaming Big Comes with a Contract

Here's the truth: Dreams don't work unless you do. Too many people romanticize ambition. They love the vision board but resist the discipline. They want the spotlight but not the late nights, the rejection, or the lonely seasons required to get there. Confidence doesn't come from hoping it will work out. It comes from knowing you will work it out. Ambition without action is anxiety.

Why Big Dreams Make People Nervous

When you share your big dream with someone, observe their reaction carefully.

- Some will be inspired.
- Some will be skeptical.
- Some will feel threatened because your dream reminds them of the one they abandoned.

And sometimes, the dream is so big that even people who love you panic. Parents, spouses, or friends might try to protect you by pulling you back toward what feels safe. However, safety and destiny rarely coexist in the same space.

From Impossible to Inevitable

Before the four-minute mile was broken, doctors said the human heart couldn't handle that speed. They were sure it was physically impossible—until Roger Bannister did it. The same year he broke the record, three other athletes also achieved it. Not because the human body suddenly evolved, but because once one person proved it was possible, everyone else's confidence expanded overnight. That's the power of a big dream: it doesn't just liberate you—it liberates everyone watching.

The Dream Is Free. The Work Is Not.

Here's the part people don't like: Big dreams come with hefty price tags.

- Time.
- Focus.
- Energy.
- Rejection.
- Failure.
- Repetition.

Most people love the idea of success until they see the invoice attached to it. But here's the upside: once you've paid the price, nobody can repossess the confidence that comes from knowing you *earned* it.

Key Takeaways from Chapter Three

- The phrase *"be realistic"* kills more dreams than failure ever will.
- Other people's limits don't have to become your ceilings.
- Big dreams require significant work—there's no shortcut.
- Fear often masquerades as wisdom. Call it out.
- Every dreamer pays a price. Confidence comes from knowing you can afford it.

CHAPTER FOUR:
The Confidence Contract–Do the Work

Why Real Confidence is Built on Preparation, Not Pretending

There's a moment every ambitious person eventually faces: A big idea. The dream is clear. The excitement is real. But then comes the grind–the unglamorous, repetitive, lonely work required to make it real. This is where most people quit. Not because they lack talent or ambition, but because they lack the stamina to keep going when the applause stops and the results take longer than expected. Here's the truth: **Confidence isn't built on dreams. It's built on discipline.**

Why Talent Alone is Never Enough

We've all seen it:

- The gifted athlete who never makes it past high school.
- The brilliant student who never turns potential into progress.
- The charismatic entrepreneur who starts big but burns out fast.

Talent creates attention. Work ethic creates empires. As the saying goes, *"Hard work beats talent when talent doesn't work hard."* Confidence isn't the belief that things will magically work out. It's the certainty that you've done the work to handle whatever comes next.

The Silent Contract Behind Every Success

Every confident person you admire has signed an invisible contract with themselves. It reads: *I will not quit before I master this. I will pay the price in time, energy, focus, and repetition until the result matches the vision.* You can't fake this contract. Your confidence knows whether you've signed it or not. That's why impostor syndrome thrives when preparation is missing. Deep down, you know when you haven't earned it yet. Real confidence says, *'I belong here because I've done the work to be here.'*

Beyoncé and the Myth of Overnight Success

People love to talk about Beyoncé's success—the Grammys, the tours, the global influence. But here's what they forget: she once said she rehearsed 16 hours a day for months preparing for a single performance. She released albums while touring, trained her voice while exhausted, and treated every stage like an audition for the next one. Her success isn't magic. It's math: *hours of preparation × relentless consistency = world-class confidence.*

Why Shortcuts Steal Confidence

The world loves shortcuts. Quick fame. Overnight money. Easy results. But shortcuts come with side effects:

- You get the stage before you've built the skill.
- You get the opportunity before you have the discipline to handle it.
- You get the recognition before you have the resilience to keep it.

And then imposter syndrome creeps in because deep down, you know you skipped steps. Real confidence comes from the reps, not the spotlight.

The Integrity of Effort

Here's something most people don't realize: Confidence isn't just emotional—it's ethical. When you cut corners, you betray yourself. Your brain keeps receipts. You can post the highlight reel online, but internally, you know when you haven't earned it. On the other hand, when you've done the work—when you've sacrificed, prepared, studied, rehearsed, and repeated—you walk into the room differently. Not arrogantly. Not timidly. But with the quiet, unshakable confidence of someone who knows they've paid in full.

The Daily Deposit Rule

High performers don't wait for perfect timing or motivation. They treat confidence like a bank account:

- **Every workout** is a deposit.
- **Every practice session** is a deposit.
- **Every rejection you learn from** is a deposit.
- **Every uncomfortable risk you take** is a deposit.

By the time the big moment arrives—the pitch, the performance, the promotion—you're not hoping you'll rise to the occasion. You're cashing in on every deposit you've made along the way.

Key Takeaways from Chapter Four

- Talent opens the door. Work ethic keeps it open.
- Confidence comes from preparation, not pretending.
- Every successful person has signed the *"Do the Work"* contract.
- Shortcuts create impostor syndrome. Repetition builds mastery.
- Daily deposits of effort compound into unshakable confidence.

CHAPTER FIVE:
Fear, Failure, and the Courage to Try Again

Why the Most Successful People Fail the Most–and Keep Going Anyway

Let's get something straight: the difference between people who win big and those who stay stuck isn't talent, money, or luck. It's courage. Specifically, the courage to fail, learn, and try again when things don't go as planned. Most people see failure as final. High performers see it as feedback. That single perspective shift separates dreamers from doers, talkers from leaders, and amateurs from experts.

The Fear Equation

Fear shows up in three predictable ways:

1. **Fear of failure** – *"What if I try and it doesn't work?"*
2. **Fear of judgment** – *"What will people say about me if I fail?"*
3. **Fear of inadequacy** – *"What if I'm not good enough to pull this off?"*

These questions feel reasonable. But here's the truth: **fear isn't a sign to stop. It's a signal you're aiming at something meaningful.** If there's no fear, there's probably no growth on the other side of it.

F.E.A.R. Has Two Meanings

An old acronym says fear can mean two things:

- **Forget Everything And Run**
- **Face Everything And Rise**

The choice between those two defines your future. The reality is that *you can play it safe your whole life and still fail.* Jobs disappear. Economies collapse. Industries change overnight. Playing small doesn't protect you from failure; it only guarantees you never experience your full potential.

The Power of Public Failure

Some of the most iconic names in business and entertainment failed publicly before they succeeded:

- **Steve Jobs** was fired from Apple, the company he co-founded, before coming back years later to turn it into the most valuable brand in the world.
- **Oprah Winfrey** was told she wasn't "fit for television."
- **Michael Jordan** was cut from his high school basketball team.
- **Walt Disney** went bankrupt before building his empire.

They didn't just fail. They failed where everyone could see it.

But here's the thing: people forget the failures once you win. And the confidence you gain from getting back up becomes unshakable because you know nothing can destroy you permanently unless you quit.

Rejection is Redirection

One of the most freeing lessons in life is realizing that **'no' isn't the end—it's often the best guidance you'll ever get.** Rejection teaches two critical things:

1. Sometimes the door closes because it wasn't your door.
2. Sometimes it closes because you need to grow before you can handle what's on the other side.

Either way, the confident person doesn't stop at the first 'no.' They take the feedback, refine their approach, and knock again—smarter, better, bolder.

Fail Fast. Learn Faster.

The most innovative companies in the world—Google, Amazon, SpaceX—operate on a principle called *"failing fast."* They experiment constantly. They expect things to break. They see mistakes as tuition, not tragedy. Why? Because the faster you fail, the faster you learn. And the faster you learn, the faster you succeed.

How to Build Courage on Demand

Confidence doesn't eliminate fear. It gives you the tools to act despite it. Here's how high performers do it:

- **They expect fear.** It's part of the process, not a problem to solve.
- **They break risks into small steps.** Big goals shrink when you focus on the following action, not the entire mountain.

- **They collect evidence of resilience.** Every time you recover from a setback, you prove to yourself you can survive the next one.

Courage compounds like interest—the more you practice it, the stronger it gets.

The Courage Dividend

When you face fear and failure repeatedly, something amazing happens:

- Your risk tolerance grows.
- Your recovery time shortens.
- Your confidence skyrockets because you trust yourself to handle anything.

At that point, the fear never entirely goes away—but it loses its power to control you. And that's when you become unstoppable.

Key Takeaways from Chapter Five

- Fear signals growth, not danger—act anyway.
- Failure is feedback. Use it, don't fear it.
- Rejection often redirects you to something better.
- Courage compounds over time. The more you face fear, the less power it has over you.
- The people who win the biggest often failed the most on the way there.

CHAPTER SIX:
The Confidence Cost

Why Real Success Always Sends You the Bill

Everyone loves the *idea* of success. The spotlight. The applause. The freedom. The influence. But here's what doesn't make it to the Instagram highlight reel: **success always sends you a bill before it delivers the benefits.** And the cost isn't always measured in dollars.

- It costs comfort.
- It costs time.
- It costs relationships.
- It costs the illusion of safety that most people cling to their entire lives.

This is why confidence matters so much. If you're not confident, the first taste of sacrifice will convince you to quit.

The Beyoncé Rule: Rehearse Longer Than Anyone Applauds

Everyone wants to be a legend on stage. Few want to rehearse like one. Beyoncé famously rehearsed for months—up to 16 hours a day—for a single Coachella performance. That's why when she walks on stage, there's no panic, no self-doubt, no "I hope this works." She's not guessing. She's already paid for that moment in sweat, time, and discipline. That's why her confidence feels unshakable. It *is* unshakable—because it was built in private long before the public ever saw the results.

The Myth of the Easy Win

We live in a culture obsessed with shortcuts:

- "Passive income."
- "Overnight success."

- "Life hacks."

But there's nothing passive about real wealth, influence, or impact. Behind every "overnight success" is a decade of work nobody clapped for.

Here's what most people don't get: **shortcuts create shaky confidence.** Because deep down, you know when you haven't paid the full price. You feel it in your gut when the opportunity outpaces your preparation. That's why so many people self-sabotage after early wins—they don't actually trust themselves to sustain success.

The Hidden Costs No One Talks About

Success often requires:

- **Lonely seasons** when you're building while others are partying.
- **Uncomfortable conversations** about money, vision, and boundaries.
- **Letting go of relationships** that want the old version of you to stay the same.

- **Endless rejection and revision** before the breakthrough finally comes.

That's the part people don't see on social media. The grind rarely gets likes. But here's the paradox: *those costs are what create the confidence to handle the reward.*

Why Paying the Price Builds Unshakable Confidence

When you've done the work, paid the price, and sacrificed for the goal:

- Nobody can tell you that you didn't earn it.
- Nobody can make you feel like an impostor.
- Nobody can shake your belief in yourself because you already passed the tests they didn't see.

Confidence built on comfort collapses under pressure. Confidence built on cost becomes unbreakable.

The Illusion of Safety

Most people trade their dreams for the illusion of safety.

- The "secure job."
- The "guaranteed paycheck."
- The "stable routine."

But here's the truth: industries collapse. Companies fold. Technology replaces entire careers overnight. Safety isn't absolute. The people who thrive in uncertain times aren't the ones who stayed comfortable–they're the ones who learned to adapt, take risks, and remain confident even when the ground beneath them shifted.

The Legacy Question

Here's the final cost that ambitious people eventually face: Do you want comfort now, or legacy later? Because you rarely get both. Every entrepreneur, leader, and changemaker who built something that outlived them paid a price for it—early mornings, late nights, misunderstood seasons, public failures, private doubts. However, the legacy makes the price worthwhile.

Key Takeaways from Chapter Six

- Success sends the bill before it delivers the benefits.
- Shortcuts create shaky confidence; sacrifice builds unshakable confidence.
- Safety is often an illusion. Growth lives outside comfort zones.
- The price you pay in private shows up as confidence in public.
- Legacy always costs more than convenience—but pays forever.

CHAPTER SEVEN:
Rejection is Direction

How to Turn Every 'No' into Power, Clarity, and Forward Motion

Every ambitious person faces rejection. A failed pitch. An ignored proposal. An opportunity that never calls back. For most people, rejection feels personal. It stings. It shuts them down. It convinces them to shrink their dreams to avoid feeling that sting again. But for high performers, rejection isn't a stop sign. It's a signal. **Rejection doesn't just block the wrong path—it points you toward the right one.**

Why 'No' Feels So Heavy

Rejection cuts deep because it attacks three things at once:

1. **Your idea** – It feels like the concept you believed in wasn't good enough.
2. **Your effort** – It feels like all the work you put in didn't matter.
3. **Your identity** – It makes you wonder if *you* aren't good enough.

But here's the truth: rejection isn't about your worth. It's about alignment. Sometimes the timing, audience, or platform isn't right yet.

The Michael Jordan Lesson

When Michael Jordan got cut from his high school basketball team, the story could have ended there. He could have believed the coach's 'no' was final. Instead, he decided it was feedback. He trained harder, studied the game obsessively, and came back so dominant that his coach looked foolish for ever doubting him. That's what high performers do: they turn rejection into fuel instead of failure.

The Gift of Clarity

Rejection gives you three things if you're willing to look for them:

1. **Clarity about fit** – Maybe this wasn't your audience, market, or opportunity. Now you know.
2. **Clarity about skill gaps** – Maybe you need to develop, refine, or pivot before the next attempt.
3. **Clarity about resilience** – Maybe you're committed to the goal or simply interested in it.

Most people never discover the next level of their talent because they let the first 'no' be the final one.

Rejection Creates Decision Points

When you get rejected, you have three options:

- **Retreat** – Shrink the dream to avoid future pain.
- **Repeat** – Keep trying the same thing in the same way and call it persistence.
- **Refine** – Take the feedback, make adjustments, and come back stronger.

Confident Confidence always chooses the third option.

The $22,000 'No'

Years ago, I asked a senior manager to approve my budget for a professional certification. He said no. Not because I wasn't capable, but because he didn't think it was worth the money. So I paid for it myself.

Six months later, that certification landed me a job offer paying $22,000 more than I was making under him. That one 'no' changed the trajectory of my entire career—and it wouldn't have happened if I'd taken his rejection as the final word.

The Paradox of Rejection

The doors that close often teach you more than the ones that open.

- Getting turned down for one deal might push you toward a better one.
- Not getting the job might force you to start the business you were meant to run.
- Losing one opportunity might free you to pursue the one you were truly built for.

Rejection refines ambition. It clarifies calling. It exposes where you've outgrown old environments.

How to De-Personalize 'No'

High performers train themselves to separate rejection from identity. Here's how:

- **See the bigger picture.** Maybe this isn't a 'no' forever. It's a 'no' for now.
- **Detach your worth.** A rejected idea doesn't mean a rejection of you.
- **Extract the lesson.** Ask what this 'no' makes possible that a "yes" might have prevented.

That mental shift turns rejection from something that stops you into something that sharpens you.

Key Takeaways from Chapter Seven

- Rejection isn't personal; it's directional.
- Every 'no' reveals either a better path, a skill gap, or a timing issue.
- The most successful people use rejection as fuel, not failure.

- Doors that close often prepare you for the ones that open later.
- Detach your identity from outcomes. Let 'no' shape you, not shrink you.

CHAPTER EIGHT:
The Confidence Economy

Why Confidence is the Most Valuable Currency You Own

Money moves when confidence does. In business. In leadership. In sales. In negotiations. People buy into people before they buy into products. They follow leaders before they follow visions. They invest in confidence before they invest in companies. That's why confidence isn't just a feeling—it's economic power.

The Invisible Currency of Success

When you walk into a boardroom, pitch a new idea, or lead a team through uncertainty, people make decisions about you in seconds.

- *Do they trust you?*
- *Do they believe you can deliver?*
- *Do they feel safe betting on you?*

The answer to those questions often has nothing to do with your resume—and everything to do with the confidence you project.

Confidence and Closing Deals

Sales experts know this: The first thing you sell is yourself. The product, the price, the features—they matter. But if you sound unsure, apologetic, or hesitant, the deal dies before you ever get to the details. Confidence is contagious. It makes people lean in. It signals: *"I believe in this so much I'm willing to stake my name on it."*

That belief often matters more than the bullet points in your presentation.

Why Investors Bet on Confidence

Venture capitalists will tell you: They're not just betting on ideas—they're betting on founders. Two people can pitch the same concept. One projects fear, doubt, and uncertainty. The other projects have clarity, passion, and confidence. Guess who gets the funding? The confident entrepreneur might not have all the answers yet, but investors know they'll figure it out because they trust the person behind the plan.

The Confidence–Income Connection

Here's the uncomfortable truth:

- The people making the most money aren't always the smartest.
- The people leading the most prominent companies aren't always the most talented. But they are usually the most confident.

Confident people ask for a promotion. Confident people negotiate the raise. Confident people launch their businesses, make the call, send the proposal, and take the risk. Meanwhile, hesitant people wait to "feel ready" and watch opportunities pass them by.

The Cost of Insecurity in the Marketplace

A lack of confidence shows up in measurable ways:

- Underpricing your services because you don't believe you're worth more.
- Overexplaining or apologizing in meetings instead of leading decisively.
- Hesitating to pitch ideas until someone else gets credit for them.

Insecurity leaks money, influence, and opportunities. Confidence creates them.

The Competitive Advantage of Certainty

In a noisy, distracted, competitive world, people crave certainty. That's why confidence wins.

- Customers buy from the brand that sounds sure of itself.
- Employees follow the leader who makes decisions with conviction.
- Audiences trust the speaker who owns the stage instead of begging for approval.

Confident Confidence doesn't mean arrogance. It means clarity. It means *I know what I bring to the table–and I bring it unapologetically.*

Building a Confidence-Based Brand

Your name is a brand, whether you realize it or not. Every email, meeting, presentation, and post either deposits or withdraws from your reputation account. Confidence grows this account faster than any marketing tactic because:

- It creates trust.
- It attracts opportunities.
- It accelerates influence.

In the marketplace, perception is often reality. Confidence shapes both.

Key Takeaways from Chapter Eight

- Confidence is economic power. It moves money, influence, and opportunity.
- People buy certainty, not confusion.
- Investors, customers, and employers bet on confidence before credentials.
- Insecurity leaks opportunities; confidence multiplies them.
- A confident personal brand opens doors before credentials ever speak.

CHAPTER NINE:
The Comparison Trap

How to Stop Measuring Your Worth by Someone Else's Highlights

Comparison is the silent killer of confidence. You can be making progress, breaking barriers, and building something extraordinary until you scroll through social media or hear someone else's success story. Suddenly, what felt like enough doesn't feel like much at all. That's the trap: **comparison turns your race into someone else's scoreboard.**

The Highlight Reel Illusion

Social media shows the vacation, not the debt. The wedding photo, not the arguments. The award, not the years of rejection that came before it. When you compare your *behind-the-scenes* to someone else's *highlight reel,* you will always feel behind. Confidence evaporates because you're measuring your reality against their marketing.

The Myth of the "Best"

We love labels like *The Greatest of All Time* in sports, business, and entertainment.

- Who's the best basketball player ever?
- Who's the greatest singer alive?
- Who's the top entrepreneur of the decade?

But here's the problem: greatness isn't a competition—it's a contribution. Michael Jordan didn't need to be LeBron James. Whitney Houston didn't need to be Beyoncé. They each brought something unique to the table that didn't require comparison to be valuable. Confident Confidence says, **I don't have to be the best. I have to be the only one who can do what I do the way I do it.**

Why Comparison Steals Confidence

Comparison creates three toxic beliefs:

1. *"I'm behind."*
2. *"I'm not good enough."*
3. *"I need to do what they're doing to win."*

Those beliefs push people into copying trends, chasing validation, and abandoning their own lane—all because they're trying to keep up with someone else's story. And nothing kills confidence faster than pretending to be someone you're not.

The Danger of Trend-Chasing

Every industry has its "hot" trends: crypto, AI, TikTok, real estate, and so on. Trends aren't bad.

But when you chase them out of insecurity instead of strategy, you lose twice:

- First, because you're late to the trend.
- Second, because you abandoned the thing that made you unique in the first place.

Confidence stays rooted. It doesn't panic when someone else's path is getting attention. It knows *my lane will pay off if I keep running it*.

From Competition to Collaboration

Confident people don't see competition as a threat. They see it as confirmation that the market is big enough for everyone. There are over 56 million millionaires on this planet. There is no shortage of money, success, or opportunity. The insecure mindset says, *"If they win, I lose."* The confident mindset says, *"If they win, it proves winning is possible."*

How to Stay in Your Lane

1. **Define your metrics.** Decide what success means for *you,* not the internet.
2. **Limit comparison triggers.** Unfollow accounts or mute voices that fuel insecurity.
3. **Celebrate your own wins.** Even small progress deserves recognition.
4. **Admire without envy.** Let other people's success inspire you, not shame you.

Confidence grows when you stop auditioning for someone else's approval.

The Freedom of Authenticity

When you stop competing for attention and start creating from authenticity, everything changes:

- Your work gets better.
- Your opportunities multiply.
- Your confidence skyrockets because you're no longer living someone else's story.

The loudest people online often crave attention. The most confident people often create impact quietly—and the world eventually can't ignore it.

Key Takeaways from Chapter Nine

- Comparison turns your race into someone else's scoreboard.
- Confidence collapses when you measure your worth against trends or timelines.
- Greatness isn't competition; it's contribution.
- Stay in your lane. Let success be personal, not comparative.
- Authenticity always outlasts attention.

CHAPTER TEN:
The Confidence Blueprint

A Practical Framework for Building Unshakable Confidence

We've talked about rejection. We've talked about fear, failure, and risk. We've talked about comparison, criticism, and the cost of chasing greatness. However, it's now time to make this practical. Confident Confidence isn't just a concept to admire. It's a system you can live by–a blueprint you can follow so that confidence becomes your natural state, not an occasional feeling. Here's the framework.

Step One: Decide Who You Are

Confidence starts with identity, not income. If you tie your confidence to titles, achievements, or applause, you'll spend your life chasing validation instead of building value. Instead, you must decide who you are before the world gives you a label. Ask yourself:

- What do I stand for?
- What won't I compromise?
- What does success look like *for me*, not for anyone else?

Because when you know who you are, you stop letting fear, failure, or other people's opinions write your story.

Step Two: Master One Thing First

Confidence grows fastest where competence grows first. Pick one skill, one business, or one goal—and get world-class at it. The marketplace pays a premium for specialists, not generalists. More importantly, mastering one thing proves to you that you can go from amateur to expert. That proof creates the internal confidence to tackle bigger goals later.

Step Three: Build the Courage Muscle

Confidence isn't the absence of fear. It's the habit of moving forward despite it. Treat courage like a muscle:

- Start small.
- Take one uncomfortable action daily.
- Gradually increase the size of your risks.

Over time, what used to scare you becomes normal—and that's how you expand your capacity for bigger dreams.

Step Four: Reframe Failure as Feedback

Every 'no,' every setback, every wrong turn—it's all data. Confident Confidence turns pain into instruction:

- What worked?
- What didn't?
- What needs to change next time?

Failure only defines you if you refuse to learn from it.

Step Five: Protect Your Environment

Confidence leaks in toxic environments. If you're constantly surrounded by negative voices, comparison traps, or people who belittle your ambitions, your confidence will erode—even if you're talented. Protect your energy. Build circles that challenge you to grow but refuse to let you shrink.

Step Six: Practice Publicly

Don't wait until you feel ready before you show up.

- Post the content.
- Launch the product.
- Pitch the idea.
- Take the shot.

Every time you practice in public, your confidence expands. You stop living for permission and start living on purpose.

Step Seven: Define Success on Your Terms

Confident Confidence isn't about looking successful—it's about feeling fulfilled. Decide what matters most to you:

- Freedom?
- Impact?
- Legacy?
- Creativity?

Let those values guide your decisions so you're not chasing someone else's definition of winning.

The Daily Confidence Checklist

Here's a simple routine to build Confident Confidence every day:

1. **Morning Affirmation:** Remind yourself who you are before the world tries to tell you.
2. **One Bold Action:** Do something outside your comfort zone before noon.
3. **Gratitude + Wins:** Document three things you did well today, no matter how small.
4. **Next Step:** End the day by deciding the following action for tomorrow.

Small, consistent wins stack into unstoppable confidence over time.

Living with Confident Confidence

When you put all of this together, something powerful happens:

- Rejection doesn't derail you.
- Fear doesn't freeze you.
- Comparison doesn't control you.
- Failure doesn't define you.

You stop waiting for perfect conditions or universal approval. You start moving through life with the quiet, unshakable certainty that *this will work because I will make it work.* That's Confident Confidence.

Key Takeaways from Chapter Ten

- Identity first, achievement second.
- Mastery builds confidence faster than motivation.
- Courage compounds when practiced daily.

- Failure is data, not destiny.
- Define success for yourself–or someone else will.

CHAPTER ELEVEN:
The Weight of Confidence

Let's be honest. There's a different kind of confidence that shows up when you lose fifty pounds and slip into a suit that no longer feels like it's holding its breath for dear life. Weight loss is about much more than looks. It's about energy, stamina, and the way you carry yourself when you feel good inside and out.

Confidence has always been about more than vanity—it's about the way you show up in the world. And whether we like it or not, the world often responds to you based on how you present yourself. When your appearance meets the demand of the task at hand, doors open; you're no longer just "there" in the room—you *own* the room.

The Hard Truth

For me, this transformation began when I was over 350 pounds. Now, let's get one thing straight: I was no bum. I was neat, clean, well-dressed, and carried myself with pride. People saw a man who appeared well-groomed. But inside, I knew the truth—my health was holding me back.

Then came the conversation that hit me harder than a treadmill on level ten. A man I deeply respected looked at me one day and said, **"You are not profitable."** At first, those words felt like a slap in the face. Profitable? Who says that to someone? But I never forgot them. As time passed, they became a turning point in my life. He wasn't talking about money—he was talking about me. My energy, my health, my ability to fully perform in business, family, relationships, and life.

The weight I carried for my height was literally decreasing my opportunities to show up at full capacity. I wasn't lazy. I wasn't unmotivated. I was an active, hardworking husband, father, and business leader. But I was performing at 70% when I had the potential to perform at 100%.

Life in the Heavy Lane

I remember trying to play with my young children and running out of breath too quickly. They'd be laughing and sprinting around the yard while I was standing there, pretending to admire the scenery so that I could catch my breath. I remember walking around Disney World with my family and needing to sit down because my knees and back were protesting with every step. Long family road trips? We had to make extra stops so I could stretch, walk around, and keep my body from locking up.

I was present. I was at the games, school events, birthdays, and celebrations. But I knew I wasn't showing up at my best. And the worst part? I could feel it affecting my confidence.

An Honest Conversation

Then came another conversation—this one with my physician. He leaned back in his chair, looked at me seriously, and said: **"Carrying this much weight doesn't just affect your heart, your joints, and your blood pressure. It affects your sex life too."**

I raised my eyebrows.

He continued, "Blood flow is everything. A poor diet, lack of physical activity, and excess weight can all affect circulation. And if blood isn't flowing the way it should, nothing else is either."

He didn't sugarcoat it. Obesity is tied to issues like low testosterone, reduced stamina, and decreased performance in the bedroom.

He looked at me squarely and said, "**If you lose the weight, you improve the blood flow. If**

you improve the blood flow, let's just say confidence isn't the only thing that *rises*." It was blunt. It was slightly embarrassing. But it was true.

The Sexual Benefit of Weight Loss

Nobody talks about this enough, but let's be real—weight loss affects your energy, stamina, and confidence in intimacy.

- Your energy levels go up.
- Your confidence goes up.
- Your willingness to plan date night goes up because you're not worried about fatigue or performance issues.

There's a reason doctors talk about cardiovascular health and sexual health in the same conversation: they're connected. When your heart and circulation improve, everything improves.

Be Willing to Take Advantage of Assistance

Here's something I had to learn the hard way: you don't have to do it alone. Some people can change their diet and hit the gym to see results quickly. Others have genetics or health conditions that make it much harder. Today, certain medications can help regulate appetite, metabolism, and energy levels. Some medical procedures and surgeries can significantly improve someone's health when traditional methods are insufficient. And there's no shame in that.

Too many people think needing help means weakness, when in reality, it takes confidence to say, **"I need professional guidance here."** Your journey might look different from someone else's. Maybe it's medication. Maybe it's surgery. Maybe it's a personal trainer. Maybe it's all three. But the goal is the same—health, energy, and confidence that fills every room you walk into.

The Confidence Curve

And that's when it hit me—weight loss doesn't just change how the world sees you. It changes how you see yourself. For a white-collar executive, it might be the difference between nervously tugging at your shirt during a keynote and striding across the stage like you were born to be there. For a blue-collar worker, it might mean finishing an eight-hour shift with enough energy left to play with your kids afterward instead of collapsing on the couch. For entrepreneurs, it might mean having the stamina to chase investors, lead their team, and still attend networking events without appearing exhausted. When the scale drops, your confidence rises. Not because you look like a fitness model, but because you feel capable again.

Closing the Chapter with Confidence

Whether you wear a hard hat, a tailored suit, or run your empire in sweatpants from home, weight loss can skyrocket your confidence, health, and opportunities—in every room of your life. It's not about chasing perfection—it's about aligning how you feel on the inside with how you show up on the outside. Because when you look the part, feel the part, and believe you belong, the world tends to agree.

And here's the thing: **you're not alone in this journey.** There are people everywhere with the same goal—to become the strongest, healthiest, most confident version of themselves. When you connect with a community working toward the same vision, your commitment multiplies, your accountability deepens, and your wins feel even more significant.

Reading this chapter means you've already taken the first step. You've faced the reality, embraced the possibility of change, and decided you're worth the effort. That deserves to be celebrated. So here's a bold statement to put on your mirror, your fridge, your desk—anywhere you'll see it every day: **"My body will no longer**

hold my confidence hostage. I control my health, my energy, and my future." Say it until you believe it. Then believe it until you live it.

CHAPTER TWELVE:
Confident Confidence in High-Pressure Environments

Let's face it—some workplaces feel like you've walked onto the set of *Survivor*. Alliances form. Strategies shift. People smile at you in the hallway while secretly eyeing the promotion you both want. And whether you're climbing the corporate ladder, running a non-profit, or building your own business from scratch, the pressure can feel relentless.

But here's the truth: **pressure doesn't have to crush you—it can create you.** Diamonds are only formed under intense pressure, and leaders who master Confident Confidence in competitive environments shine brighter, last longer, and win bigger than those who crack under the weight.

Corporate Confidence: Thriving in the Shark Tank

Corporate life is not for the faint of heart. The stakes are high, the deadlines are tight, and the competition can feel ruthless. People want the promotion, the corner office, the bigger budget, the international assignment. If you're not careful, you'll spend so much energy comparing yourself to everyone else that you'll forget to showcase the unique value you bring to the table. **Confident Confidence says:** "I don't compete by copying others. I compete by maximizing what only I can bring."

Take *Carla*, for example. She worked for a Fortune 500 company where everyone seemed to have an MBA, a LinkedIn following the size of a small country, and a side hustle consulting business. Instead of panicking, Carla doubled down on what made her unique—her ability to deliver complex projects *without drama*. While others scrambled to appear busy, she remained calm, met every deadline, and built a reputation for reliability under pressure. When the leadership team needed someone to manage a high-visibility, high-risk project, who did they call? The woman who made pressure look easy. In high-pressure corporate settings, competence matters. But *composure*? That's what gets you promoted.

Non-Profit Confidence: Competing for Impact

Non-profit work can feel like corporate life with less pay, more passion, and twice the politics. The competition here isn't just for funding and visibility—it's for credibility. Every grant, every donor, every partnership matters. Leaders who thrive in this space don't just have confidence in their mission; they have Confident Confidence in their ability to *adapt, influence, and inspire*, no matter the circumstances.

For example, a friend of mine once ran a youth mentorship non-profit. While other leaders fought over the same small pool of donors, he expanded his network into corporate sponsorships, city partnerships, and even collaborations with his so-called "competitors." He turned rivals into allies by focusing on *impact over ego*. His mantra? "If I stay focused on the mission, the money will find me." That's Confident Confidence in action—knowing that excellence attracts resources, opportunities, and people who want to be part of something bigger than themselves.

Entrepreneurs: Confidence in the Marketplace Jungle

Entrepreneurship? Oh, that's a different beast. Here, competition isn't just the person in the next cubicle. It's every business owner in your industry fighting for the same clients, the same investors, and the same slice of attention in a noisy marketplace. And while competition can feel cutthroat, the truth is **that competition validates**

your idea. Nobody is copying a business that isn't making money. But here's the catch— entrepreneurs need a special kind of Confident Confidence: the ability to stay bold in the face of rejection while constantly innovating.

Consider *Marcus*, who opened a small coffee shop in a city already drowning in Starbucks stores. Instead of panicking, he leaned into what made him different—live music nights, locally roasted beans, and a "pay what you can" policy once a month for struggling families. He didn't compete on size; he competed on experience. Within a year, his shop was the place where culture, coffee, and community collided.

In business, **confidence sells as much as competence.** People buy energy, vision, and leadership just as much as they purchase products and services.

Surviving Cutthroat Environments

Some environments prioritize speed over strategy and quantity over quality.

- The loudest person gets the attention.
- The most aggressive team gets the funding.
- The fastest talker gets the client.

But here's the secret: *the professional who stays poised under pressure ultimately wins the long game.* I once heard an executive say, *"I don't hire the person who talks the most in meetings. I hire the one who speaks last with the clearest solution."* Confident Confidence doesn't rush to prove itself. It doesn't crumble under criticism. It doesn't need to win every small argument because it's focused on winning the big picture.

Humor in the Hustle

Let's be honest–some workplaces are so serious they feel allergic to laughter. But humor, when used wisely, is a secret weapon in competitive environments. When everyone else is tense, the leader who can diffuse the room with a clever comment or a calm smile earns the trust of those around them. People follow leaders who make them *feel* something positive, not just those who hit the quarterly metrics.

One CEO I know keeps a sign on his desk that says, *"I'm not stressed. I'm just pre-successful."* He swears it keeps him sane in back-to-back meetings.

Preparing for Elevation

High-pressure environments require preparation, not just ambition. You can't just want the promotion, the partnership, or the funding—you have to be ready for it. That means:

- Mastering your craft so completely that excellence becomes your baseline.
- Building relationships before you need them so opportunities feel like partnerships, not favors.

- Staying so consistent that when your big moment comes, no one is surprised—you've been operating at that level for months.

Confident Confidence doesn't beg for a seat at the table. It builds a reputation so strong that when you arrive, people say, *"What took so long?"*

Bold Statements for Your Desk, Fridge, or Mirror

1. **"Pressure makes diamonds. I'm here to shine."**
2. **"I don't compete to survive. I compete to dominate."**
3. **"Calm is my superpower in a chaotic world."**
4. **"I don't chase opportunities. I come prepared so they chase me."**
5. **"Confidence isn't arrogance; it's excellence without apology."**

Final Thoughts

Whether you're in a corporate boardroom, a non-profit strategy session, or building your business from scratch, high-pressure environments are inevitable. But pressure doesn't have to crush you. With Confident Confidence, it can refine you, promote you, and position you for levels of success that even the most frantic competitors will never reach. Because at the end of the day, people follow the professional who stays calm, competent, and confident—even when the whole room feels like it's on fire.

CONCLUSION:
Living with Confident Confidence

If you've made it this far, give yourself some credit—you've just taken a masterclass in becoming the most confident version of yourself. Not the loud, fake-it-till-you-make-it kind of confidence, but the kind that sticks even when life tries to knock the wind out of you.

And here's the thing about confidence—it's like a muscle. Reading this book once is like going to the gym for a single workout and expecting a six-pack by tomorrow morning; that's not going to happen. You have to **keep coming back**, keep strengthening it, and keep reminding yourself of the tools, examples, and truths you've read here.

I'll never forget when I was told, "You are not profitable." I didn't laugh then—it stung—but looking back, it was probably the most profitable conversation I ever had because it pushed me to level up in ways I didn't even know I needed. That's the beauty of confidence work: the process doesn't always feel good, but the results are worth it. Confidence is not built in one moment; it is built daily.

As you revisit the lessons in this book, remember that **Confident Confidence** is a practice that requires ongoing attention and effort. Return to these chapters whenever life shakes your certainty or when fear whispers that you are not enough. Let this book remind you that rejection, risk, and setbacks are part of the process—and they are powerless against a person full of Confident Confidence.

Decide to be that person in your workplace, your business, your family, and your circle of influence. Let your confidence be the anchor that steadies you, the fuel that drives you, and the light that inspires others. Read these pages often, apply the principles consistently, and become the person whose confidence cannot be shaken.

Life will continue to throw high-pressure boardrooms, long nights, competitive workplaces, health challenges, and moments of self-doubt your way. That's normal. But now, you have the blueprint for handling it all with **Confident Confidence**—the kind that says, *"I've got this because I will make this work."*

Here's my advice:

- **Refer to this book often.** Don't just read it once and let it collect dust.
- **Put the bold statements on your mirror, your desk, or your fridge.** Confidence grows faster when you see and say the right things daily.

- **Laugh a little along the way.** Some chapters may have hit hard, but confidence also grows when you stop taking yourself so seriously.

Most importantly, know this: I'm sure the steps outlined in this book will assist you as you navigate your path. They worked for me, they've worked for countless others, and they will work for you if you put them into practice.

So here's your final bold statement to carry forward: **"I am the CEO of my confidence. Every room I enter, every challenge I face, every goal I pursue—I own it all."** Now go out there and *live* it.

www.ingramcontent.com/pod-product-compliance
Lightning Source LLC
Chambersburg PA
CBHW071353160426
42811CB00094B/283